Texting While Driving
for Geniuses

By 4dham J. Henders8

www.justforgeniuses.com

DISCLAIMER: The book is a work of parody. Nothing in this book is meant to imply any facts about any actual persons or entities.

All rights reserved. No part of this publication may be reproduced, distributed, or transmitted in any form or by any means, including photocopying, recording, or other electronic or mechanical methods, without the prior written permission of the publisher.

Copyright © 2014 by Westlake Gavin Publishers LLC

Just for Geniuses, For Geniuses, and accompanying logos are trademarks of Westlake Gavin Publishers LLC and may not be used without written permission. All other trademarks are the property of their respective owners. Westlake Gavin Publishers LLC, is not associated with any other product or service mentioned in this book.

HUMANS OF MIRTH COLLECTION   TGGT1000

Library of *Con*-gress Cataloging-in-Publication Data

Texting While Driving for Geniuses / by 4dham J. Henders8.
p. cm.
ISBN 978-1-63231-998-2
1. Henders8, 4dham J.   2. Parody, imitations, etc.   I. Title.

10 9 8 7 6 5 4 3 2 1

Inside...

How to weave all over the road like a pro.

Outwit mean police officers who want to ensure public safety (whatever that is.)

The right way to handle the situation if you ever get caught. Hint: it's never your fault.

How you can "Up the ante" for even more fun. Such as: running red lights, changing lanes without signaling, and so much more...

Texting While Driving *for Geniuses*

Please, please, before someone ends up **dead** or **seriously injured**, stop fiddling with your mobile phone and concentrate on the road. Don't put your fellow drivers, pedestrians, and innocent children at risk.

The life you save may be your own.

Texting While Driving *for Geniuses*

Please, please, before someone ends up **dead** or **seriously injured**, stop fiddling with your mobile phone and concentrate on the road. Don't put your fellow drivers, pedestrians, and innocent children at risk.

The life you save may be your own.

Read enough? Turn to page 104.

Texting While Driving *for Geniuses*

Please, please, before someone ends up **dead** or **seriously injured**, stop fiddling with your mobile phone and concentrate on the road. Don't put your fellow drivers, pedestrians, and innocent children at risk.

The life you save may be your own.

Read enough? Turn to page 104.

Please, please, before someone ends up **dead** or **seriously injured**, stop fiddling with your mobile phone and concentrate on the road. Don't put your fellow drivers, pedestrians, and innocent children at risk.

The life you save may be your own.

Read enough? Turn to page 104.

Texting While Driving *for Geniuses*

Texting While Driving *for Geniuses*

Please, please, before someone ends up **dead** or **seriously injured**, stop fiddling with your mobile phone and concentrate on the road. Don't put your fellow drivers, pedestrians, and innocent children at risk.

The life you save may be your own.

Read enough? Turn to page 104.

Texting While Driving *for Geniuses*

Please, please, before someone ends up **dead** or **seriously injured**, stop fiddling with your mobile phone and concentrate on the road. Don't put your fellow drivers, pedestrians, and innocent children at risk.

The life you save may be your own.

Read enough? Turn to page 104.

Texting While Driving *for Geniuses*

Please, please, before someone ends up **dead** or **seriously injured**, stop fiddling with your mobile phone and concentrate on the road. Don't put your fellow drivers, pedestrians, and innocent children at risk.

The life you save may be your own.

Read enough? Turn to page 104.

Texting While Driving *for Geniuses*

Please, please, before someone ends up **dead** or **seriously injured**, stop fiddling with your mobile phone and concentrate on the road. Don't put your fellow drivers, pedestrians, and innocent children at risk.

The life you save may be your own.

Read enough? Turn to page 104.

Texting While Driving *for Geniuses*

Please, please, before someone ends up **dead** or **seriously injured**, stop fiddling with your mobile phone and concentrate on the road. Don't put your fellow drivers, pedestrians, and innocent children at risk.

The life you save may be your own.

Read enough? Turn to page 104.

Texting While Driving *for Geniuses*

Please, please, before someone ends up **dead** or **seriously injured**, stop fiddling with your mobile phone and concentrate on the road. Don't put your fellow drivers, pedestrians, and innocent children at risk.

The life you save may be your own.

Read enough? Turn to page 104.

Texting While Driving *for Geniuses*

Please, please, before someone ends up **dead** or **seriously injured**, stop fiddling with your mobile phone and concentrate on the road. Don't put your fellow drivers, pedestrians, and innocent children at risk.

The life you save may be your own.

Read enough? Turn to page 104.

Texting While Driving *for Geniuses*

Please, please, before someone ends up **dead** or **seriously injured**, stop fiddling with your mobile phone and concentrate on the road. Don't put your fellow drivers, pedestrians, and innocent children at risk.

The life you save may be your own.

Read enough? Turn to page 104.

Texting While Driving *for Geniuses*

Please, please, before someone ends up **dead** or **seriously injured**, stop fiddling with your mobile phone and concentrate on the road. Don't put your fellow drivers, pedestrians, and innocent children at risk.

The life you save may be your own.

Read enough? Turn to page 104.

Texting While Driving *for Geniuses*

Please, please, before someone ends up **dead** or **seriously injured**, stop fiddling with your mobile phone and concentrate on the road. Don't put your fellow drivers, pedestrians, and innocent children at risk.

The life you save may be your own.

Read enough? Turn to page 104.

Texting While Driving *for Geniuses*

Please, please, before someone ends up **dead** or **seriously injured**, stop fiddling with your mobile phone and concentrate on the road. Don't put your fellow drivers, pedestrians, and innocent children at risk.

The life you save may be your own.

Read enough? Turn to page 104.

Texting While Driving *for Geniuses*

Texting While Driving *for Geniuses*

Please, please, before someone ends up **dead** or **seriously injured**, stop fiddling with your mobile phone and concentrate on the road. Don't put your fellow drivers, pedestrians, and innocent children at risk.

The life you save may be your own.

Read enough? Turn to page 104.

Texting While Driving *for Geniuses*

Please, please, before someone ends up **dead** or **seriously injured**, stop fiddling with your mobile phone and concentrate on the road. Don't put your fellow drivers, pedestrians, and innocent children at risk.

The life you save may be your own.

Read enough? Turn to page 104.

Texting While Driving *for Geniuses*

Please, please, before someone ends up **dead** or **seriously injured**, stop fiddling with your mobile phone and concentrate on the road. Don't put your fellow drivers, pedestrians, and innocent children at risk.

The life you save may be your own.

Read enough? Turn to page 104.

Texting While Driving *for Geniuses*

Please, please, before someone ends up **dead** or **seriously injured**, stop fiddling with your mobile phone and concentrate on the road. Don't put your fellow drivers, pedestrians, and innocent children at risk.

The life you save may be your own.

Read enough? Turn to page 104.

Texting While Driving *for Geniuses*

Please, please, before someone ends up **dead** or **seriously injured**, stop fiddling with your mobile phone and concentrate on the road. Don't put your fellow drivers, pedestrians, and innocent children at risk.

The life you save may be your own.

Read enough? Turn to page 104.

Texting While Driving *for Geniuses*

Please, please, before someone ends up **dead** or **seriously injured**, stop fiddling with your mobile phone and concentrate on the road. Don't put your fellow drivers, pedestrians, and innocent children at risk.

The life you save may be your own.

Read enough? Turn to page 104.

Please, please, before someone ends up **dead** or **seriously injured**, stop fiddling with your mobile phone and concentrate on the road. Don't put your fellow drivers, pedestrians, and innocent children at risk.

The life you save may be your own.

Read enough? Turn to page 104.

Texting While Driving *for Geniuses*

Please, please, before someone ends up **dead** or **seriously injured**, stop fiddling with your mobile phone and concentrate on the road. Don't put your fellow drivers, pedestrians, and innocent children at risk.

The life you save may be your own.

Read enough? Turn to page 104.

Texting While Driving *for Geniuses*

Texting While Driving *for Geniuses*

Please, please, before someone ends up **dead** or **seriously injured**, stop fiddling with your mobile phone and concentrate on the road. Don't put your fellow drivers, pedestrians, and innocent children at risk.

The life you save may be your own.

Read enough? Turn to page 104.

Texting While Driving *for Geniuses*

Please, please, before someone ends up **dead** or **seriously injured**, stop fiddling with your mobile phone and concentrate on the road. Don't put your fellow drivers, pedestrians, and innocent children at risk.

The life you save may be your own.

Read enough? Turn to page 104.

Texting While Driving *for Geniuses*

Please, please, before someone ends up **dead** or **seriously injured**, stop fiddling with your mobile phone and concentrate on the road. Don't put your fellow drivers, pedestrians, and innocent children at risk.

The life you save may be your own.

Read enough? Turn to page 104.

Texting While Driving *for Geniuses*

Texting While Driving *for Geniuses*

Please, please, before someone ends up **dead** or **seriously injured**, stop fiddling with your mobile phone and concentrate on the road. Don't put your fellow drivers, pedestrians, and innocent children at risk.

The life you save may be your own.

Read enough? Turn to page 104.

Texting While Driving *for Geniuses*

Texting While Driving *for Geniuses*

Please, please, before someone ends up **dead** or **seriously injured**, stop fiddling with your mobile phone and concentrate on the road. Don't put your fellow drivers, pedestrians, and innocent children at risk.

The life you save may be your own.

Read enough? Turn to page 104.

Texting While Driving *for Geniuses*

Please, please, before someone ends up **dead** or **seriously injured**, stop fiddling with your mobile phone and concentrate on the road. Don't put your fellow drivers, pedestrians, and innocent children at risk.

The life you save may be your own.

Read enough? Turn to page 104.

Texting While Driving *for Geniuses*

Please, please, before someone ends up **dead** or **seriously injured**, stop fiddling with your mobile phone and concentrate on the road. Don't put your fellow drivers, pedestrians, and innocent children at risk.

The life you save may be your own.

Read enough? Turn to page 104.

Texting While Driving *for Geniuses*

Please, please, before someone ends up **dead** or **seriously injured**, stop fiddling with your mobile phone and concentrate on the road. Don't put your fellow drivers, pedestrians, and innocent children at risk.

The life you save may be your own.

Read enough? Turn to page 104.

Texting While Driving *for Geniuses*

Please, please, before someone ends up **dead** or **seriously injured**, stop fiddling with your mobile phone and concentrate on the road. Don't put your fellow drivers, pedestrians, and innocent children at risk.

The life you save may be your own.

Read enough? Turn to page 104.

Texting While Driving *for Geniuses*

Please, please, before someone ends up **dead** or **seriously injured**, stop fiddling with your mobile phone and concentrate on the road. Don't put your fellow drivers, pedestrians, and innocent children at risk.

The life you save may be your own.

Read enough? Turn to page 104.

Texting While Driving *for Geniuses*

Please, please, before someone ends up **dead** or **seriously injured**, stop fiddling with your mobile phone and concentrate on the road. Don't put your fellow drivers, pedestrians, and innocent children at risk.

The life you save may be your own.

Read enough? Turn to page 104.

Texting While Driving *for Geniuses*

Please, please, before someone ends up **dead** or **seriously injured**, stop fiddling with your mobile phone and concentrate on the road. Don't put your fellow drivers, pedestrians, and innocent children at risk.

The life you save may be your own.

Read enough? Turn to page 104.

Texting While Driving *for Geniuses*

Please, please, before someone ends up **dead** or **seriously injured**, stop fiddling with your mobile phone and concentrate on the road. Don't put your fellow drivers, pedestrians, and innocent children at risk.

The life you save may be your own.

Read enough? Turn to page 104.

Texting While Driving *for Geniuses*

Please, please, before someone ends up **dead** or **seriously injured**, stop fiddling with your mobile phone and concentrate on the road. Don't put your fellow drivers, pedestrians, and innocent children at risk.

The life you save may be your own.

Read enough? Turn to page 104.

Texting While Driving *for Geniuses*

Please, please, before someone ends up **dead** or **seriously injured**, stop fiddling with your mobile phone and concentrate on the road. Don't put your fellow drivers, pedestrians, and innocent children at risk.

The life you save may be your own.

Read enough? Turn to page 104.

Texting While Driving *for Geniuses*

Please, please, before someone ends up **dead** or **seriously injured**, stop fiddling with your mobile phone and concentrate on the road. Don't put your fellow drivers, pedestrians, and innocent children at risk.

The life you save may be your own.

Read enough? Turn to page 104.

Texting While Driving *for Geniuses*

Please, please, before someone ends up **dead** or **seriously injured**, stop fiddling with your mobile phone and concentrate on the road. Don't put your fellow drivers, pedestrians, and innocent children at risk.

The life you save may be your own.

Read enough? Turn to page 104.

Texting While Driving *for Geniuses*

Please, please, before someone ends up **dead** or **seriously injured**, stop fiddling with your mobile phone and concentrate on the road. Don't put your fellow drivers, pedestrians, and innocent children at risk.

The life you save may be your own.

Read enough? Turn to page 104.

Texting While Driving *for Geniuses*

Please, please, before someone ends up **dead** or **seriously injured**, stop fiddling with your mobile phone and concentrate on the road. Don't put your fellow drivers, pedestrians, and innocent children at risk.

The life you save may be your own.

Read enough? Turn to page 104.

Texting While Driving *for Geniuses*

Texting While Driving *for Geniuses*

Please, please, before someone ends up **dead** or **seriously injured**, stop fiddling with your mobile phone and concentrate on the road. Don't put your fellow drivers, pedestrians, and innocent children at risk.

The life you save may be your own.

Read enough? Turn to page 104.

Texting While Driving *for Geniuses*

Please, please, before someone ends up **dead** or **seriously injured**, stop fiddling with your mobile phone and concentrate on the road. Don't put your fellow drivers, pedestrians, and innocent children at risk.

The life you save may be your own.

Read enough? Turn to page 104.

Texting While Driving *for Geniuses*

Please, please, before someone ends up **dead** or **seriously injured**, stop fiddling with your mobile phone and concentrate on the road. Don't put your fellow drivers, pedestrians, and innocent children at risk.

The life you save may be your own.

Read enough? Turn to page 104.

Texting While Driving *for Geniuses*

Please, please, before someone ends up **dead** or **seriously injured**, stop fiddling with your mobile phone and concentrate on the road. Don't put your fellow drivers, pedestrians, and innocent children at risk.

The life you save may be your own.

Read enough? Turn to page 104.

Texting While Driving *for Geniuses*

Please, please, before someone ends up **dead** or **seriously injured**, stop fiddling with your mobile phone and concentrate on the road. Don't put your fellow drivers, pedestrians, and innocent children at risk.

The life you save may be your own.

Read enough? Turn to page 104.

Texting While Driving *for Geniuses*

Texting While Driving *for Geniuses*

Please, please, before someone ends up **dead** or **seriously injured**, stop fiddling with your mobile phone and concentrate on the road. Don't put your fellow drivers, pedestrians, and innocent children at risk.

The life you save may be your own.

Read enough? Turn to page 104.

Texting While Driving *for Geniuses*

Please, please, before someone ends up **dead** or **seriously injured**, stop fiddling with your mobile phone and concentrate on the road. Don't put your fellow drivers, pedestrians, and innocent children at risk.

The life you save may be your own.

Read enough? Turn to page 104.

Texting While Driving *for Geniuses*

Please, please, before someone ends up **dead** or **seriously injured**, stop fiddling with your mobile phone and concentrate on the road. Don't put your fellow drivers, pedestrians, and innocent children at risk.

The life you save may be your own.

Read enough? Turn to page 104.

Yep, that's it. That's the whole book.

Honestly, how many more times do we need to repeat it? If fifty times is not enough, we suggest you read the book again. As many times as it takes.

You got the message right away? That's wonderful news, but not surprising. After all… you are a Genius!

 Use it as a notebook. (The left sided pages have been lined for your convenience.)

 "Gift it forward" Give the book to an unsuspecting friend, family member, or colleague—and help spread the message of safe driving to as many people as possible.

 Add it to your *Just for Geniuses*™ collection. No promises, but serious collectors are expecting the value of all *Just for Geniuses*™ branded merchandise to substantially rise in the decades and centuries ahead.

Texting While Driving *for Geniuses*

Nonetheless, we would like to thank you for taking the time to read this book.

We couldn't write books like this without readers like you to support us. Any feedback you give would be greatly appreciated. We have fragile egos, so be gentle about it. Or funny.

Please give us feedback at
www.justforgeniuses.com/feedback

Texting While Driving *for Geniuses*

Sorry to hear that. But don't despair. The real power of the *Just for Geniuses*™ brand is the flexibility and the ability to customize it **to your needs**. Think gifts, collectibles, promos, charity fund-raising, corporate events, advocacy, and much more.

Depending on your needs, we have the perfect solution for you:

- Submit a customization request to our design team at no cost. (We will try to accommodate everyone's request based on our discretion.)

- Ask our Professional Services team to assist you (minimum order applies.) This is necessary for time-sensitive requests.

- License *Just for Geniuses*™ for your product, service, or media needs. This would give you the most flexibility.

What are you waiting for? Submit your request today at **www.justforgeniuses.com/solutions**

www.justforgeniuses.com

www.ingramcontent.com/pod-product-compliance
Lightning Source LLC
Chambersburg PA
CBHW070854050426
42453CB00012B/2190